Yellow Stockings

Contents

Welcome to *Rigby Navigator* 2

Renewed Framework Teaching Objectives 3

How to use the *Rigby Navigator Plays* Teaching Guides 4

About the Play 6

Lesson 1 8

Lesson 2 9

Focus on (Lesson 1) 10

Focus on (Lesson 2) 11

PCM 1 12

PCM 2 13

Now Stage the Play 14

Welcome to Rigby Navigator

Giving you the Right Tools for the Job
Rigby Navigator is an easy-to-use, versatile programme specially designed to help you unlock the potential of guided reading. It has been developed to make guided reading easy to manage and enjoyable for both teachers and children. The programme provides a compact series of books for fiction, non-fiction, poetry and plays for 7–11 year olds. *Rigby Navigator* also has the flexibility to be used alongside your existing guided reading resources.

Navigator Plays
Rigby Navigator plays have been written to help you deliver creative and effective guided reading sessions for all your pupils. The plays are tailor-made for guided reading lessons, so they provide just the right amount of material and at the right interest level. There are 12 plays, three for each of year groups 3–6 (P4–7), with parts for six characters in each play. These specially written resources make classroom management easy, while giving the children the pleasure of reading complete plays.

Each play is supported by its own Teaching Guide, offering guided reading notes that provide a model for teaching. They put a wealth of ideas at your fingertips for engaging children in the reading of plays and, additionally, include notes on performing the play. The ideas may, of course, be adapted according to the needs of guided reading within your class.

A New Generation of Teacher Support
Each Teaching Guide provides two guided reading lessons. The Guides contain details on how to introduce the plays, questions to ask before, during and after reading, and suggestions for follow-up and independent work. The literacy objectives for each lesson are clearly highlighted.

Appropriate question prompts are given to encourage discussion of, for example, characterisation, setting, theme, format and the differences between prose and play script. Coverage of the Renewed Framework core learning objectives allows children to progress to the higher order reading skills of deductive, inferential and evaluative comprehension, which are essential for SATs preparation.

Differentiation
The wide range of ability levels in the classroom adds to the time needed to prepare for effective guided reading. *Rigby Navigator Plays* Teaching Guides offer teachers flexible routes through the plays so that each guided reading lesson can be differentiated. The plays have been written in sets of three around topics pertinent to each year group. Each set of plays offers a gradient of challenge in order to cater for the range within each class. *Rigby Navigator* Teaching Guides state the National Curriculum Level of each play so that guided reading lessons can be successfully differentiated.

It should be noted that reading play scripts offers some particular challenges. Children may be unfamiliar with the layout of plays in general. They will need to read the stage directions silently and interpret them in line with the text. Some plays use unfamiliar vocabulary in terms of idiom or historical setting. The need for expression, characterisation and interplay with the audience adds another dimension to the reading of these plays. For this reason, the level of the play scripts is somewhat lower than the level of straightforward fiction or non-fiction texts for a particular year group.

Children need to participate in a first run-through to familiarise themselves with the story line. The teacher will guide their interpretation and offer assistance in understanding the context for each play. The children should then have the opportunity to rehearse their own roles and then return to a collaborative re-reading and possibly play-reading performance.

Top Children's Playwrights
Rigby Navigator Plays contains well-crafted plays by respected children's writers, which will capture children's imaginations and develop them as enthusiastic readers and writers of plays.

Narrative Genre Coverage
The *Rigby Navigator* plays in each year group are linked by genre. The genre relates to one or more of the literacy units for that year:
- **Year 3:** Stories with familiar settings; Dialogue and plays
- **Year 4:** Stories with historical settings; Plays

- **Year 5:** Traditional stories, fables, myths, legends; Dramatic conventions
- **Year 6:** Fiction genres.

Models for Writing
The plays also serve as perfect exemplars for children's own writing. The Teaching Guides have a strong focus on writing, drawing on the essential link between reading and writing.

Rigby Navigator Plays and Assessment
Valuable information can be accrued during guided reading about children's application of essential reading skills and strategies. The Teaching Guides include questioning prompts to track children's level of understanding of the teaching objectives of the lesson. This will ensure that you have a clear picture of each child's progress.

Drama and Speaking & Listening
The *Rigby Navigator* plays present significant opportunities for reinforcing and extending children's developing drama, and speaking and listening skills. These include:

- preparing plays for performance or reading aloud, identifying appropriate expression, tone and volume
- developing and using specific vocabulary related to plays (e.g. role, play script, stage directions, rehearsal, performance, prop, sound effects)
- offering reasons and evidence for views; considering alternative opinions
- responding appropriately to the contributions of others in the light of differing viewpoints
- using talk to organise roles and action
- using the language of possibility to investigate and reflect on feelings, behaviour or relationships
- creating roles showing how behaviour can be interpreted from different viewpoints
- developing scripts based on improvisation
- commenting constructively on plays and performances, discussing effects and how they are achieved.

In addition to the opportunities offered within the lessons themselves, each Teaching Guide provides a double-page spread of guidance for staging and performing the play.

Renewed Framework Teaching Objectives

Yellow Stockings – Historical Settings

Lesson 1	Lesson 2
Focus on Reading Aloud with Expression	**Focus on Comic Character**
Y4 Strand 4: 1 Create roles showing how behaviour can be interpreted from different points of view	**Y4 Strand 4: 3** Comment constructively on plays and performances, discussing effects and how they are achieved
Y4 Strand 7: 1 Identify and summarise evidence from a text to support a hypothesis	**Y4 Strand 7: 2** Deduce characters' reasons for behaviour from their actions
Y4 Strand 7: 2 Deduce characters' reasons for behaviour from their actions	**Y4 Strand 8: 2** Interrogate texts to deepen and clarify understanding and response
Y4 Strand 8: 2 Interrogate texts to deepen and clarify understanding and response	**Y4 Strand 9: 1** Develop and refine ideas in writing

NOTE: The strand numbers identified in the table above refer to the Renewed Framework core learning strands. They are: **Strand 4:** Drama; **Strand 7:** Understanding and interpreting texts; **Strand 8:** Engaging with and responding to texts; **Strand 9:** Creating and shaping texts.

How to use the Navigator Plays Teaching Guides

The *Navigator* Teaching Guides offer flexible routes through the plays for guided reading. The Guides put you in control of guided reading, as you choose the routes through the material depending on the needs of your group.

Lesson 1

At a Glance
This section gives you planning support, designed to save you valuable time, by giving you an overview of the play as well as highlighting the literacy opportunities in the text.

Think
This section introduces the play to the children, familiarising them with the features and context of the play script and activating any prior knowledge and experience that they bring to the reading. It may involve talking about the way plays are set out and read, explaining difficult vocabulary or giving an overview of the content. Depending on a group's ability, some children may be able to read the play ahead of the guided reading session.

Read and Respond
In this section of the lesson, the children can predict, reflect, recall, interpret, challenge and respond to the text.

- **Question Prompts:** These questions enable the teacher to assess whether the children have understood the play. If the children have read it in advance, it's a good opportunity for them to recall the story of the play and to retrieve detail.

- **Going Deeper:** This section leads the children deeper into the text, giving them reading strategies to help them understand and interpret it. The children are encouraged to support their views with evidence from the text.

- **Focus on:** This section of the lesson focuses on a number of pages in the play and fulfils a key objective. Children re-read a portion of the play and are encouraged to use specific reading strategies while investigating the text. Often this focused questioning requires children to read between and beyond the lines of the text.

Reflect
Now the children reflect in detail on the play they have read. This is also an opportunity to consolidate the strategies used.

Follow-up
The PCM for Lesson 1 focuses on response to the text to extend and assess reading comprehension.

Challenge: Differentiation
The main stem of the lesson is the same for all children. You can choose from the range of literacy activities available – from simple recall of fact to more probing and interpretive discussion – according to the group you are taking.

As a guided reading lesson progresses faster with more able children, the Challenge sections extend the main stem of the lesson and build on the teaching that has gone before.

Lesson 2

The second guided reading lesson works in the same way as Lesson 1, but may have different learning objectives and also includes a key writing objective. The follow-up work has a writing focus, and further writing suggestions are also given.

Annotations (callouts)

- Introduces the play and activates children's prior knowledge
- A focused look at the text
- Allows teachers to check comprehension and facilitate group discussion
- Gives an overview of the play and highlights literacy opportunities – saving you time
- Encourages critical thinking
- Consolidates strategies used
- Strong link to writing in Lesson 2
- Differentiated routes through the material put you in control
- Focused follow-up ideas
- Focused question prompts
- Focus section for both lessons
- Annotated pages put you in control
- Challenge sections allow more able children to go even deeper into the text
- One reading and one writing copymaster for each play

Tricky Biscuits

Genre: Familiar setting, play
Author: Bob Wilson
Illustrator: Garry Parsons

Key Teaching Objectives

Lesson 1
Y3 Strand 1: 4 Develop and use specific vocabulary (e.g. play-related words and phrases)
Y3 Strand 7: 1 Identify the main points of sections of text
Y3 Strand 7: 2 Infer characters' feelings in fiction and consequences in logical explanations
Y3 Strand 7: 3 Identify how different texts are organised (e.g. recognise the key differences between prose and play script)
Y3 Strand 8: 2 Empathise with characters

At a Glance

Lesson 1: Focus on Features of Play Scripts
Lesson 2: Focus on Reading Aloud with Expression

In this funny play, Miss Bell and a group of five children in her class make gingerbread biscuits for parents' evening. The children make the biscuits into shapes that have something to do with their mum or dad, but all Milly wants to do is eat them!

The familiar setting of a school classroom will allow children to bring their own experience of being at school to the play. They will be able to empathise with the characters who are much like themselves and, using the dialogue, infer characters' feelings from what they say. In turn, this will enable them to develop the skill of reading aloud with expression as they take on specific roles.

The play format provides the opportunity to compare prose and play script, identifying the key features of play scripts.

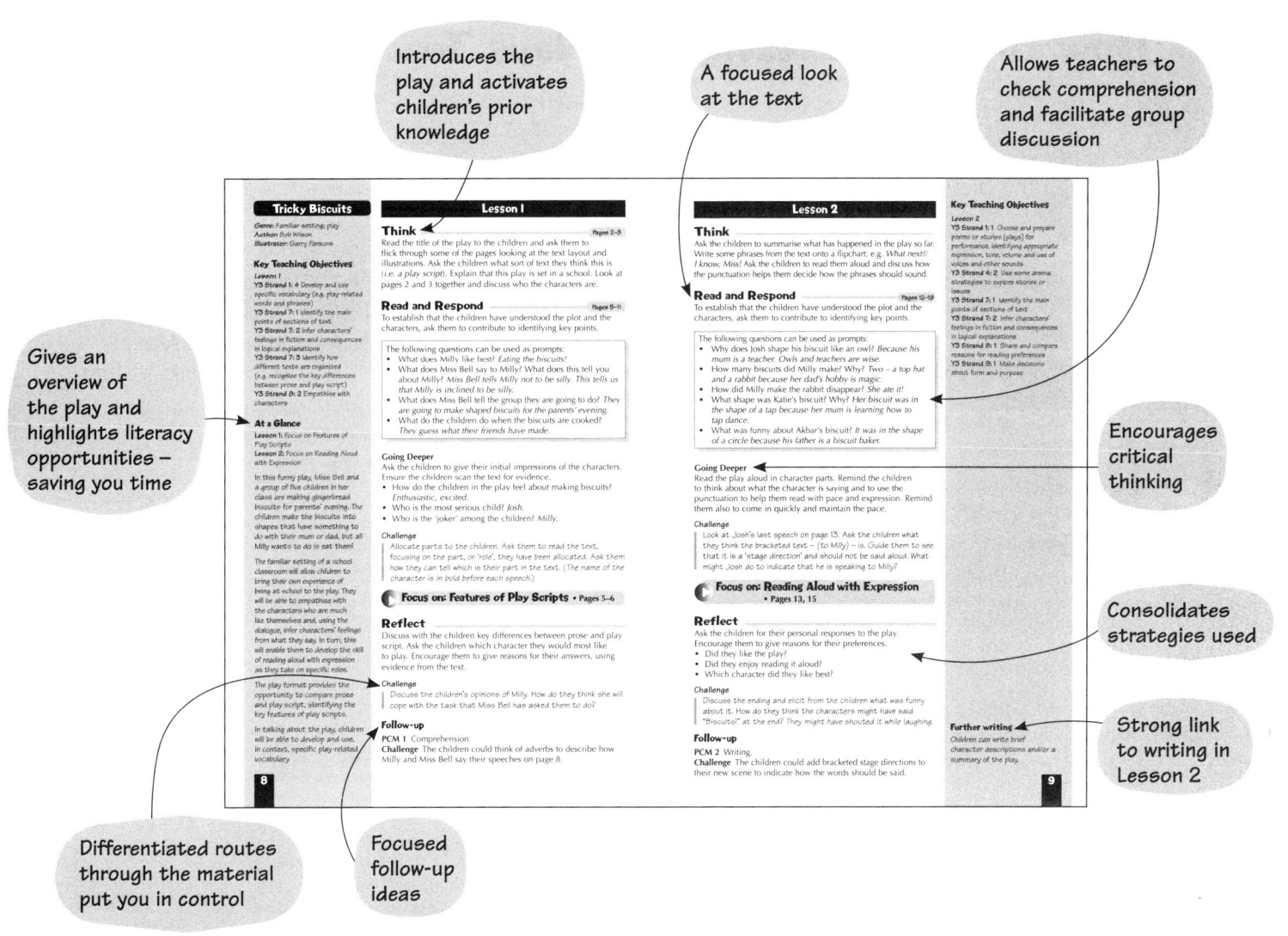

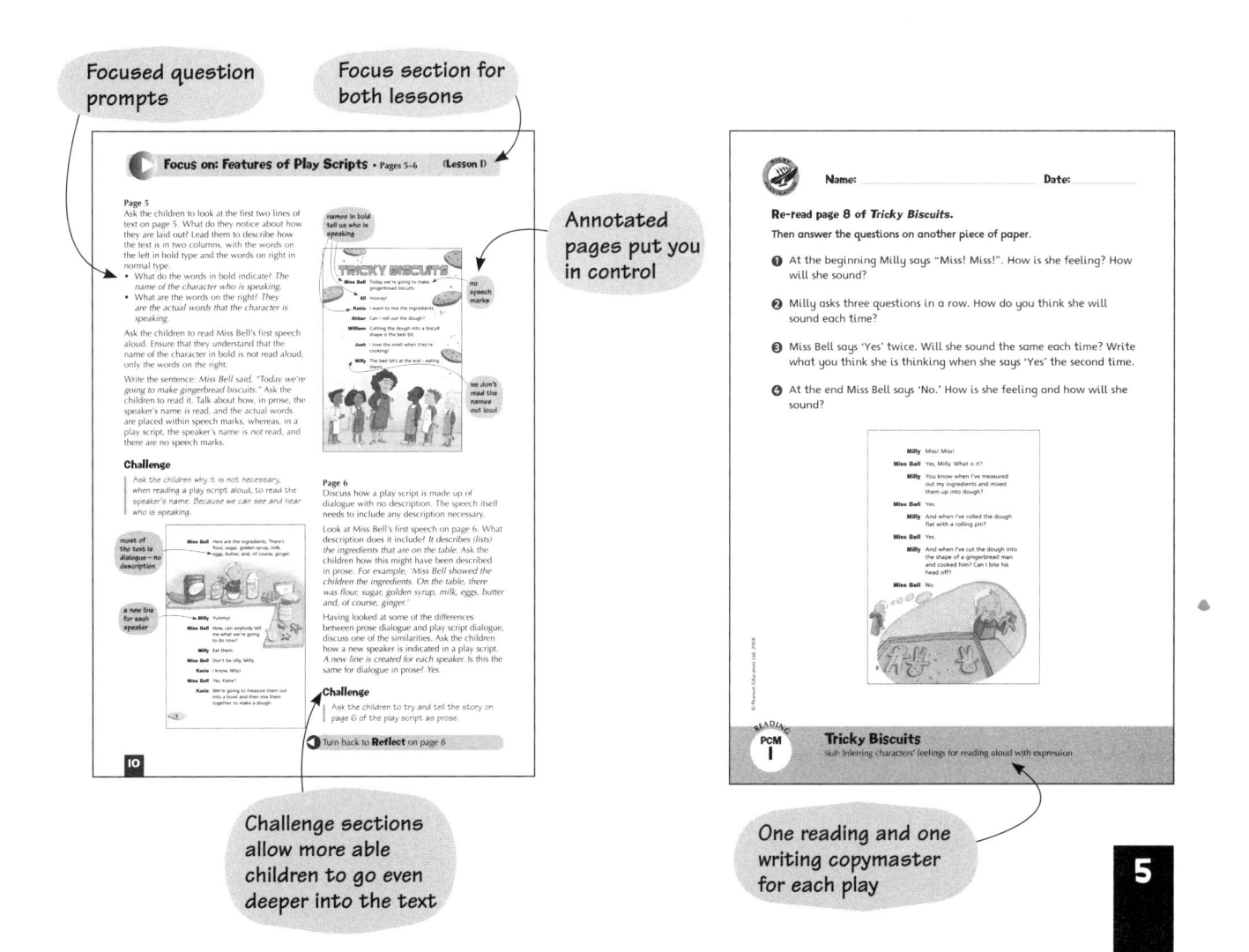

In talking about the play, children will be able to develop and use, in context, specific play-related vocabulary.

Lesson 1

Think
Pages 2–3
Read the title of the play to the children and ask them to flick through some of the pages looking at the text layout and illustrations. Ask the children what sort of text they think this is (i.e. a play script). Explain that this play is set in a school. Look at pages 2 and 3 together and discuss who the characters are.

Read and Respond
Pages 8–11
To establish that the children have understood the plot and the characters, ask them to contribute to identifying key points.

The following questions can be used as prompts:
- What does Milly like best? *Eating the biscuits.*
- What does Miss Bell say to Milly? What does that tell you about Milly? *Miss Bell tells Milly not to be silly. This tells us that Milly is inclined to be silly.*
- What does Miss Bell tell the group they are going to do? *They are going to make shaped biscuits for the parents' evening.*
- What do the children do when the biscuits are cooked? *They guess what their friends have made.*

Going Deeper
Ask the children to give their initial impressions of the characters. Ensure they scan the text for evidence.
- How do the children in the play feel about making biscuits? *Enthusiastic, excited.*
- Who is the most serious child? *Josh.*
- Who is the 'joker' among the children? *Milly.*

Challenge
Allocate parts to the children. Ask them to read the text, focusing on the part, or 'role', they have been allocated. Ask them how they can tell which is their part in the text. (*The name of the character is in bold before each speech.*)

Focus on: Features of Play Scripts • Pages 5–6

Reflect
Discuss with the children key differences between prose and play script. Ask the children which character they would most like to play. Encourage them to give reasons for their answers, using evidence from the text.

Challenge
Discuss the children's opinions of Milly. How do they think she will cope with the task that Miss Bell has asked them to do?

Follow-up
PCM 1 Comprehension.
Challenge The children could think of adverbs to describe how Milly and Miss Bell say their speeches on page 8.

Lesson 2

Think
Ask the children to summarise what has happened in the play so far. Write some phrases from the text onto a flipchart; e.g. *What next?/I know, Miss!* Ask the children to read them aloud and discuss how the punctuation helps them decide how the phrases should sound.

Read and Respond
Pages 12–15
To establish that the children have understood the plot and the characters, ask them to contribute to identifying key points.

The following questions can be used as prompts:
- Why does Josh shape his biscuit like an owl? *Because his mum is a teacher. Owls and teachers are wise.*
- How many biscuits did Milly make? Why? *Two – a top hat and a rabbit because her dad's hobby is magic.*
- How did Milly make the rabbit disappear? *She ate it!*
- What shape was Katie's biscuit? Why? *Her biscuit was in the shape of a tap because her mum is learning how to tap dance.*
- What was funny about Akbar's biscuit? *It was in the shape of a circle because his father is a biscuit baker.*

Going Deeper
Read the play aloud in character parts. Remind the children to think about what the character is saying and to use the punctuation to help them read with pace and expression. Remind them also to come in quickly and maintain the pace.

Challenge
Look at Josh's last speech on page 13. Ask the children what they think the bracketed text – (to Milly) – is. Guide them to see that it is a 'stage direction' and should not be said aloud. What might Josh do to indicate that he is speaking to Milly?

Focus on: Reading Aloud with Expression • Pages 13, 15

Reflect
Ask the children for their personal responses to the play. Encourage them to give reasons for their preferences.
- Did they like the play?
- Did they enjoy reading it aloud?
- Which character did they like best?

Discuss the ending and elicit from the children what was funny about it. How do they think the characters might have said "Biscuits!" at the end? *They might have shouted it while laughing.*

Follow-up
PCM 2 Writing.
Challenge The children could add bracketed stage directions to their new scene to indicate how the words should be said.

Further writing
Children can write brief character descriptions and/or a summary of the play.

Key Teaching Objectives

Lesson 2
Y3 Strand 1: 1 Choose and prepare poems or stories (plays) for performance, identifying appropriate expression, tone, volume and use of voices and other sounds
Y3 Strand 4: 2 Use some drama strategies to explore stories or issues
Y3 Strand 7: 1 Identify the main points of sections of text
Y3 Strand 7: 2 Infer characters' feelings in fiction and consequences in logical explanations
Y3 Strand 8: 1 Share and compare reasons for reading preferences
Y3 Strand 8: 1 Make decisions about form and purpose

Focus on: Features of Play Scripts • Pages 5–6 (Lesson 1)

Page 5
Ask the children to look at the first two lines of text on page 5. What do they notice about how they are laid out? Lead them to describe how the text is in two columns, with the words on the left in bold type and the words on right in normal type.
- What do the words in bold indicate? *The name of the character who is speaking.*
- What are the words on the right? *They are the actual words that the character is speaking.*

Ask the children to read Miss Bell's first speech aloud. Ensure that they understand that the name of the character in bold is not read aloud, only the words on the right.

Write the sentence: *Miss Bell said, "Today we're going to make gingerbread biscuits."* Ask the children to read it. Talk about how, in prose, the speaker's name is read, and the actual words are placed within speech marks, whereas, in a play script, the speaker's name is *not* read, and there are no speech marks.

Challenge
Ask the children why it is not necessary, when reading a play script aloud, to read the speaker's name. *Because we can see and hear who is speaking.*

Annotations on the page:
- names in bold tell us who is speaking
- no speech marks
- we don't read the names out loud
- most of the text is dialogue – no description
- a new line for each speaker

Page 6
Discuss how a play script is made up of dialogue with no description. The speech itself needs to include any description necessary.

Look at Miss Bell's first speech on page 6. What description does it include? *It describes (lists) the ingredients that are on the table.* Ask the children how this might have been described in prose. For example, 'Miss Bell showed the children the ingredients. On the table, there was flour, sugar, golden syrup, milk, eggs, butter and, of course, ginger.'

Having looked at some of the differences between prose dialogue and play script dialogue, discuss one of the similarities. Ask the children how a new speaker is indicated in a play script. *A new line is created for each speaker.* Is this the same for dialogue in prose? *Yes.*

Challenge
Ask the children to try and tell the story on page 6 of the play script as prose.

Turn back to **Reflect** on page 8

Name: _____ Date: _____

Re-read page 8 of *Tricky Biscuits*.

Then answer the questions on another piece of paper.

1. At the beginning Milly says "Miss! Miss!". How is she feeling? How will she sound?

2. Milly asks three questions in a row. How do you think she will sound each time?

3. Miss Bell says 'Yes' twice. Will she sound the same each time? Write what you think she is thinking when she says 'Yes' the second time.

4. At the end Miss Bell says 'No.' How is she feeling and how will she sound?

PCM 1

Tricky Biscuits
Skill: Inferring characters' feelings for reading aloud with expression

About the Play

Reading Level
This play is suitable for children reading at approximately National Curriculum Level 3C, or 5–14 Level C.

Synopsis
Yellow Stockings is set in Tudor England. It is written in natural language with a simple layout.

It is 1601 and Queen Elizabeth I is on the throne. Shakespeare's comedy *Twelfth Night* is about to open at the Globe Theatre in London, with a young boy actor named Pip playing the role of Viola. Pip's mother and his twin sister, Annie, are making the costumes for the play. Pip is due to take the finished costumes to the theatre by boat that afternoon, but Annie is still knitting a pair of gaudy yellow stockings for one of the characters. While she works, she helps Pip learn his lines, and they discuss the improbability of the *Twelfth Night* plot – which involves twins, one of whom successfully disguises herself as a boy. That couldn't happen in real life, could it? Annie promises Pip she will have the stockings done by the time he has loaded the boat, but he sets off without them. When she tries to throw them to him, he falls into the river, catches a very bad cold, loses his voice and is unable to act in the play. But Annie has an idea: she disguises herself as Pip and acts the role herself!

Characters
There are six characters in the play.
- Pip Fleet (aged 13): An actor. Chatty and cheeky.
- Annie Fleet (Pip's twin sister): Clever and a good singer. A bit jealous of Pip.
- Mistress Fleet (mother): A tailor. Anxious to please her customers. Caring mother.
- Fruit-seller: Lively, loud woman. Speaks her mind.
- Apothecary: Grumpy and serious. Thinks the theatre is a wicked place.
- Sir Perry: A bit of a dandy. Vain and foolish.

Links with Whole-class Work
This play has been selected to enable children to make informed contributions to whole-class sessions. For example:
- Children could present extracts from the play, which they have read in guided reading, to the rest of the class.

- They could discuss the way we build a picture of each character through the things that they say or do.
- They could compare play scripts and prose, focusing on how setting and characters are presented, and on how story lines are made clear. For example, in stories, the author may describe the character, whereas, in plays, the actors have to show what characters are like by the way they say their lines.
- They could perform the play for a wider audience. (See pages 14 and 15 for detailed guidance on staging the play.)
- They could discuss links between the play and their learning about the Tudors in History.

Other Navigator Plays for Year 4

- ***A Quiet Family Christmas* by Steve Barlow & Steve Skidmore**

It's Christmas Eve at Henry VIII's palace but his children won't stop squabbling. How can Catherine Parr unite the family?

- ***Light the Beacons* by Chris Buckton**

The Spanish Armada is coming to attack England and warning beacons are being lit along the coast. But will Matthew and Bess break the chain?

Yellow Stockings

Genre: Historical; play
Author: Julia Donaldson
Illustrator: Andrew Oliver

Key Teaching Objectives

Lesson 1
Y4 Strand 4: 1 Create roles showing how behaviour can be interpreted from different points of view
Y4 Strand 7: 1 Identify and summarise evidence from a text to support a hypothesis
Y4 Strand 7: 2 Deduce characters' reasons for behaviour from their actions
Y4 Strand 8: 2 Interrogate texts to deepen and clarify understanding and response

At a Glance

Lesson 1: Focus on Reading Aloud with Expression

Lesson 2: Focus on Comic Character

The play is set in Tudor England, in 1601, just as Shakespeare's comedy Twelfth Night is about to premier at the Globe Theatre in London. It focuses on a boy actor, Pip Fleet, and his twin sister, Annie. Their "impossible adventures" are rather similar to those of the twins in the Shakespeare play.

The historical setting may well support and/or anticipate study of the period in History lessons.

As the play is about plays and acting, it provides a context for discussion about play-script conventions and about how subject and form in this instance work together to enhance meaning.

If it is at all possible, give children a potted summary of Twelfth Night either before or after reading this play to enhance their appreciation.

Lesson 1

Think
Pages 2–3

Read the introduction and look at the cast list together. Explain that Shakespeare wrote *Twelfth Night*, a play in which there were twins and a character who wore yellow stockings. Explain also that in Shakespeare's time, boys played girls' parts because girls weren't allowed to act.

Read and Respond
Pages 4–15

Read up to the end of Scene Two.

> The following questions can be used as prompts:
> - What do we learn about Pip in the first scene? *Good actor (the fruit-seller cried at his last performance); cheeky (manages to get a free apple); not a good swimmer.*
> - How are Annie and Ms Fleet involved with the theatre? *Ms Fleet is a tailor and she and Annie help to make costumes.*
> - Why is Annie jealous of Pip? *She would like to be able to act as well.*
> - Why aren't the yellow stockings ready on time? *Annie doesn't like knitting them – she was testing Pip on his lines.*
> - Why does Annie refer to what happens in Mr Shakespeare's play as "impossible adventures"?
> - What do you think will be the consequence of Pip falling into the water?

Going Deeper
Allocate parts to the children. Remind them to use the punctuation to help them read with pace and expression.

Challenge
Ask one of the children to be Annie and put him/her in the hot seat. Ask the others to put questions to her.

Focus on: Reading Aloud with Expression
• Pages 9–10

Reflect
Discuss with the children how understanding a character can help in reading aloud with appropriate expression.

Challenge
Ask the children to predict what might happen next. Has the writer given us any clues?

Follow-up
PCM 1 Comprehension.
Challenge The children could retell Scene One in the first person, from the Fruit-seller's point of view.

Lesson 2

Think
Ask the children to summarise what has happened so far, and to explain the relevance of yellow stockings.

Read and Respond
Pages 16–22

To establish that the children have understood the plot and the characters, ask them to contribute to identifying key points.

> The following questions can be used as prompts:
> - What has happened to Pip? *As a result of his falling in the water, he has become ill and lost his voice.*
> - What was Annie's idea and why was it daring? *To take Pip's place; girls were not allowed to act.*
> - What is funny about Sir Perry's line "I know the Fleet family well"? *He obviously doesn't know them all that well because he doesn't recognise Annie playing Viola.*
> - Why do you think Sir Perry changed his mind about the yellow stockings after seeing the play? *Because the character who wore yellow stockings in* Twelfth Night *was a silly idiot.*
> - How do you think Pip felt about not being able to perform on opening night? Do you think his feelings were mixed?

Going Deeper
Explore further Annie's idea to stand in for Pip. Ask the children if they were surprised by what she did. Discuss the clues the writer left in the first two scenes.

Challenge
Discuss the theme of gender discrimination in Tudor times and how things differ now.

 Focus on: Comic Character • Pages 7–8, 19–20

Reflect
Ask the children for their personal responses to the play. Encourage them to give reasons for their preferences.
- Did they like the play? Which character did they like best?
- What do they think might have happened if someone had spotted that Viola was played by a girl?

Challenge
Discuss the fact that the play is 'historical fiction'. Which aspects do the children think are factual, and which fiction? Did they learn anything about the historical period?

Follow-up
PCM 2 Writing.
Challenge Children can write a diary entry for Pip on his feelings the night that *Twelfth Night* opened at The Globe.

Key Teaching Objectives
Lesson 2
Y4 Strand 4: 3 Comment constructively on plays and performances, discussing effects and how they are achieved
Y4 Strand 7: 2 Deduce characters' reasons for behaviour from their actions
Y4 Strand 8: 2 Interrogate texts to deepen and clarify understanding and response
Y4 Strand 9: 1 Develop and refine ideas in writing

Further writing
Children can write a diary entry for Annie describing her feelings about finally acting on stage.

Focus on: Reading Aloud with Expression (Lesson 1)
• Pages 9–10

Explain to the children that you are going to be looking at what characters say to determine how the words should be read aloud with expression.

Ask the children to scan pages 9–10.
- Can they summarise what is going on? *Annie and Pip are talking about the plot of Shakespeare's* Twelfth Night.
- What sort of 'talk' is it? Lead them to conclude that it is a not-too-serious argument about the believability of the plot.
- What might characterise this kind of dialogue? *For example, it might be fast-paced, with each character picking up on what the other has said quickly, and perhaps with voices that get louder.*

Ask the children to look at Ms Fleet's speech at the top of page 9.
- How do they think she is feeling? *She's fed up with Annie's complaining. She's in a hurry to leave and wants to be sure that Annie will act responsibly while she's gone.*
- How might the reader say this speech? *Perhaps impatiently, while quickly bustling out.*

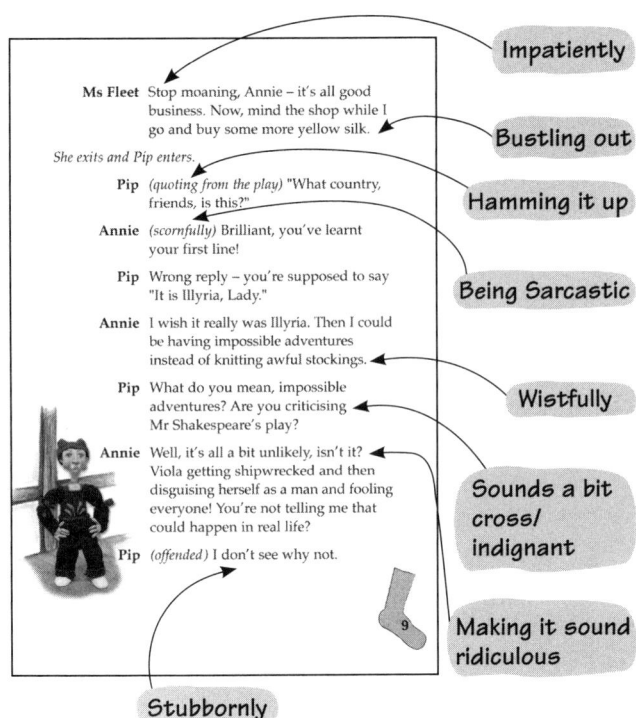

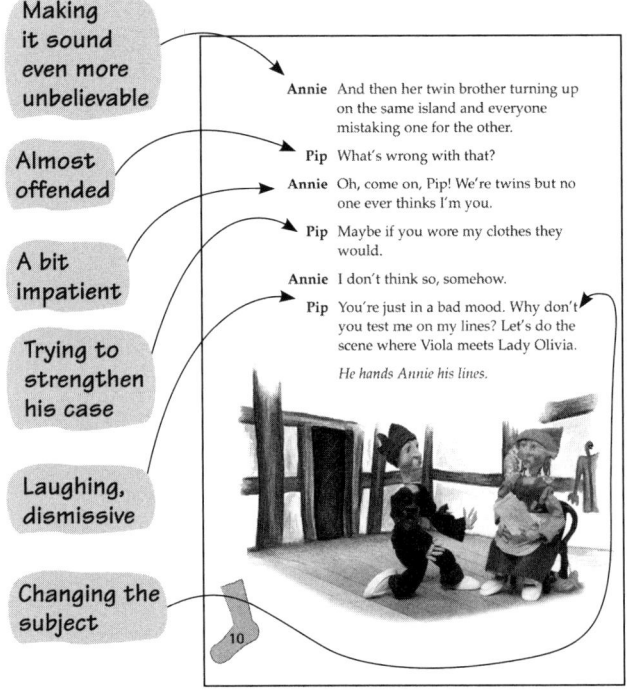

When Pip enters, he is quoting lines from the play. How might these be read? *To emphasise that he is 'acting' he could exaggerate, hamming it up, with expansive gestures.*

When Annie says "Brilliant…", is she being sincere? How should she say this speech? *No, she means exactly the opposite; she is being sarcastic.*

How is Annie feeling when she says "I wish it really was Illyria"? How do you know? *She is feeling wistful. The word "wish" indicates this, as well as the sentence that follows.*

Look at the other speeches on these two pages and ask the children to indicate how they might be said and why. Discuss how each character is responding to another's previous speech. Point out the importance of listening as well as speaking in reading a play aloud.

Challenge

Ask the children to read Annie's last speech on page 9 with and without the punctuation. This will demonstrate its importance.

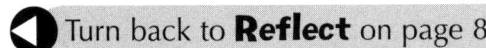 Turn back to **Reflect** on page 8

Focus on: Comic Character • Pages 7–8, 19–20 (Lesson 2)

Explain to the children that you are going to look at how the writer conveys the character of Sir Perry. First, ask them for their opinions of the character. Did they like him? Why or why not? Brainstorm words and phrases that describe Sir Perry.

Ask the children to look back at the cast list (page 3) and to read the description of Sir Perry. Now ask them to quickly skim-read pages 7 and 8 again to look for evidence to support the description.

- Why is Sir Perry unhappy about the sleeves of the doublet (close-fitting jacket) that Ms Fleet is making for him? *They are not fashionable; he wants wrist ruffs instead of turned back cuffs.*
- Why does he want the ruffs in yellow? *Because they will be bright and dazzling and get him noticed at court.*
- What is funny about the fact that he also wants a pair of yellow stockings like the ones Annie is knitting? *Annie has just commented on how horrible the yellow is and how no one in their right mind would want to wear the stockings. Yet Sir Perry assumes they are fashionable (must be if a character in the play wears them)!*

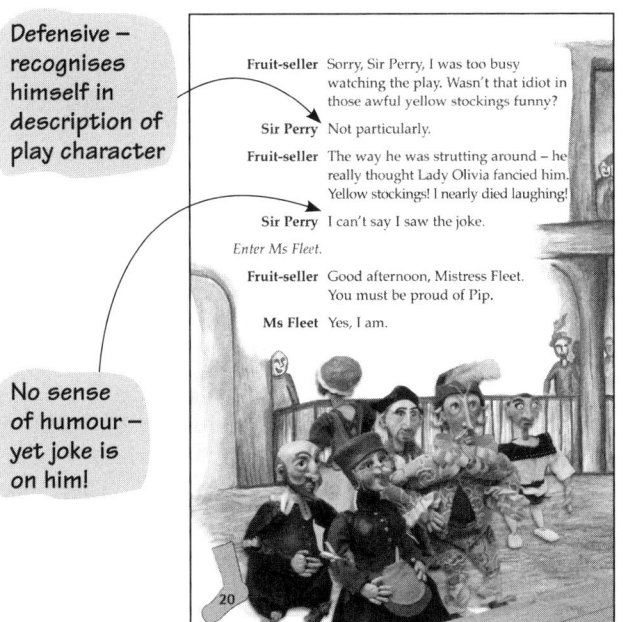

- "I never miss a new play", says Sir Perry. Why is this funny? *Because for him, the only reason for going to the theatre is to show his "fashionable" clothes off – not to enjoy the new play.*

Now turn to pages 19 and 20. Why do the children think Sir Perry might have preferred the last play? *We learn that the foolish character in the play is the one dressed in yellow stockings. So, in a way, this play has made a fool of Sir Perry.* Ask the children to explain how Sir Perry's speeches on these two pages help to further portray him as a comic character. Use the annotated pages as prompts where appropriate.

If there is time in this session – or perhaps later – ask children to undertake the same activity with pages 21 and 22.

Challenge

> Discuss how a character can be considered comic by the audience, even though he may not consider himself comic. The comedy comes from the fact that the character is unaware how foolish or silly they are. Do the children know of any characters like that in other plays or stories they have seen or read?

Turn back to **Reflect** on page 9

Name: _____ **Date:** _____

> Read the extract below. Using coloured pens, mark on the extract the places where you think the characters have to carry out an action or move in a certain way.
>
> Next to each speech, write a short note to show how an actor should say the words (*quickly, sadly* etc.).
>
> Two examples have been done for you.

Pip	Hey! I'm supposed to say that. *(Turning to Annie, annoyed)*
Annie	I know; I was just prompting you. *(Laughing)* Honestly, Pip, I think I know these lines better than you do!
	Enter Mistress Fleet.
Ms Fleet	Annie, stop prancing around with that veil. You know it's for the play.
Annie	I'm just testing Pip on his lines.
Ms Fleet	Haven't you learnt them yet, Pip? You're leaving it a bit late in the day.
Pip	Well, what about your costumes? They don't seem to be ready. Annie's still knitting those yellow stockings.
Annie	It's your fault for making me test you on your lines. Anyway, I'm on the last row. I'll have finished by the time you've loaded the other clothes into the boat.
Ms Fleet	Can you manage them all, Pip?
Pip	I'll have to, won't I?

© Pearson Education Ltd, 2008

Yellow Stockings
Skill: Annotating text to show actions and how lines should be read

Name: _____ **Date:** _____

Read Scene 4, on pages 18 to 22. Now write it as a story. The opening lines have been done for you. Finish it on the back of the sheet.

> The first performance of *Twelfth Night* was a great success. Annie played the role of Viola so well that nobody realised she had taken Pip's place. When the play was over, the fruit-seller turned to Sir Perry, who was splendidly dressed in the yellow stockings Annie had made for him . . .

Yellow Stockings

Skill: Writing play script scene as story

PCM 2

Now Stage the Play

These notes are designed to suggest ways in which the script may be brought to life in performance, rather than just read as a text. How you use them will obviously depend on whether you are staging the play to be performed in front of a wider audience, or whether you intend the children to use the "Ready, steady, act!" notes from their play scripts to develop a performance by themselves, maybe in guided reading sessions.

Suggestions have been given for props, costumes and production techniques, but many are optional. There is still great value in performing the play without too much practical effort however limited your resources may be.

What you will need
- simple costumes such as cloaks, hats and waistcoats
- apples on a tray or in a basket
- a pair of bright yellow stockings – could be football socks
- some paper or a booklet to represent a play script
- a piece of fabric for Olivia's veil
- an armful of clothes/costumes
- an apothecary's tray with a few bottles etc.

Choosing the parts
How you cast the play will depend on whether you are expecting the children to learn lines or to read the play while acting. You may want to give parts with more lines to children who will cope better.

The main acting challenge in *Yellow Stockings* is Sir Perry's role as the foppish gentleman.

You may wish to audition and choose carefully for this part, bearing in mind that he is a figure of fun and will need to be willing to 'show-off'.

There are only six parts in this play. If you wish to include the rest of the class you could:
- have a group give a short presentation about Shakespeare or The Globe Theatre
- have a group responsible for costumes and props
- ask a group or individual to direct the play
- use a group to be the Globe audience
- open the play with a variety of street sellers and town-folk.

Characters
Explain to the children that *becoming* a character can teach us a great deal more about that character than just reading the part aloud.
- Walking in the style of a character is really useful. Ask them to walk as a police officer, a ballet dancer, a triumphant footballer etc. Then ask them to walk like Sir Perry, who might be saying, "Is my doublet ready?"
- Discuss how Annie might feel knowing that she cannot perform in the theatre because she is a girl and then how she feels when she gets the chance.

Setting the scene
The action takes place in four locations – a London street, a tailor's shop, Pip's bedroom and the Globe Theatre. You may wish use signs or one key prop to start each scene.
- The opening scene could be exciting and lively involving many children. Ask them to choose a character and create a Tudor street scene.
- For Scene Four, the Globe, the audience should be bustling and settling before the performance begins.

Speaking and Moving

Speaking
Look at the cast list on pages 2 and 3 and discuss the character notes.
- Sir Perry is affected and arrogant. How might this affect his speaking voice?
- The other characters could be played with a London accent. Practise saying the opening apple rhyme in a variety of dialects.

Moving
As this play is split into four distinct scenes, encourage the actors to enter and exit on cue and in character.
- Have the children practise a bustling market street atmosphere for the opening of the play.
- Sir Perry's walk should reflect his "foppish" personality – straight backed, nose in the air, one arm floating.
- How can Pip show that he is wet? Practise dripping without the water.

Evaluating the Performance

		Teachers	Pupils
Drama Objectives	Create roles showing how behaviour can be interpreted from different viewpoints	Did the acting show Annie's frustration and Sir Perry's arrogance? Were you convinced that the apothecary was against all forms of theatre?	How did the children feel about Annie not being allowed to act on the stage? How do they think her mother feels when she does?
	Develop scripts based on improvisation	Does the children's writing reflect what actually happened in the improvisation lesson? (See 'Further Ideas' below.)	Did you feel as if you were in a Tudor theatre?
	Comment constructively on plays and performances, discussing effects and how they are achieved	Children could interview a partner and feedback their opinions to the whole group.	Ask the cast to reflect on their own performances.

Further Ideas

- Improvise a scene where the audience at the Globe arrive, argue, jostle for position and talk throughout the play about what they are seeing. Develop a script from this.
- Watch a version of *Twelfth Night*.
- Design a new outfit for Sir Perry based around the violet stockings.

Rigby
Halley Court, Jordan Hill, Oxford, OX2 8EJ
Rigby is an imprint of Pearson Education Limited, a company incorporated in England and Wales, having its registered office at Edinburgh Gate, Harlow, Essex, CM20 2JE.
Registered company number: 872828

www.rigbyed.co.uk

Rigby is a registered trademark of Elsevier, Inc, licensed to Pearson Education Limited

© Chris Buckton and Pearson Education Ltd, 2008

First published 2008

All rights reserved. The material in this publication is copyright. Pupil sheets may be freely photocopied for classroom use in the purchasing institution. However, this material is copyright and under no circumstances may copies be offered for sale. If you wish to use the material in any way other than that specified you must apply in writing to the publishers.

Yellow Stockings Teaching Notes   ISBN 978 0 433011 82 8
Yellow Stockings 6 pack with Teaching Notes   ISBN 978 0 433011 07 1

12 11 10
10 9 8 7 6 5 4 3 2

Series Editors for original version: Chris Buckton, Jean Kendall and Alison Price
Original teaching notes written by Chris Buckton
This version written by Gina Nuttall with Lesley Ford, Mike Levy and Alison MacDonald
National Curriculum levelling by Suzanne Baker and Shirley Bickler
Illustrated by Garry Parsons (page 5) and Andrew Oliver
Logo artwork by Max Ellis
Typeset by Planman Technologies, India
Printed in Malaysia, CTP-KHL